David Greig was born ... ...ue
Europe, *The Architect*, ...*...ulator*, *The Cosmonaut's
Last Message to the Woman He Once Loved in the
Former Soviet Union*, *Outlying Islands*, *San Diego*,
Pyrenees, *The American Pilot* and *Damascus*. In 1990
he co-founded Suspect Culture to produce collaborative,
experimental theatre work. His work with Suspect Culture
includes *One Way Street*, *Airport*, *Timeless*, *Mainstream*,
Casanova, *Lament* and *8000 M*. His translation of
Caligula was presented at the Donmar Warehouse in an
award-winning production in 2003, and his version of
The Bacchae was staged at the Edinburgh Festival and
on tour in 2007. His work for children and young people
includes *Danny 306 + Me Forever*, *Petra*, *Dr Korczak's
Example*, *Gobbo* and an adaptation of *Tintin in Tibet*,
presented by the Young Vic at Christmas 2005.

also by David Greig

OUTLYING ISLANDS
SAN DIEGO
THE AMERICAN PILOT
PYRENEES
DAMASCUS

translations
CALIGULA
THE BACCHAE

with Suspect Culture
CASANOVA

Published by Methuen

DAVID GREIG PLAYS: I
(*Europe, The Architect, The Cosmonaut's Last Message
to the Woman He Once Loved in the Former Soviet Union*)

VICTORIA

DAVID GREIG

Yellow Moon

The Ballad of Leila and Lee

faber and faber

First published in 2006
by Faber and Faber Limited
Bloomsbury House, 74–77 Great Russell Street,
London WC1B 3DA

This revised reprint 2007

Typeset by Country Setting, Kingsdown, Kent CT14 8ES
Printed and bound by CPI Group (UK) Ltd, Croydon, CR0 4YY

A CIP record for this book
is available from the British Library

ISBN 978-0-571-23928-3

For my companions on the
Aonach Eagach Ridge

10/9/2006

*Thanks to Alan Wilkins for his insights
into secondary school life in Fife, and to
Mike Greig, whose knowledge and ideas
regarding life on a Highland estate
were invaluable in shaping this play.*

*Thanks to Nicola McCartney, Paul Blair,
Gabriel Quigley, Gary Collins
and Kirsten Hazel Smith
for workshopping the piece with me.*

*Finally, thanks to Peter, Fiona and all the
staff at St George's West Café in Edinburgh
for making me feel so welcome during
the writing process.*

Yellow Moon was commissioned by TAG Theatre Company and premiered in the Citizens' Theatre, Circle Studio, Glasgow, on 29 September 2006. The play ran at this venue for two weeks before touring schools across Scotland. In 2007 *Yellow Moon* appeared at the Traverse Theatre as part of the Edinburgh Festival Fringe and at the Citizens' Theatre, Glasgow, before touring. The cast for both tours was as follows:

Nalini Chetty
Keith MacPherson
Beth Marshall
Andrew Scott-Ramsay

Director Guy Hollands
Music Nigel Dunn
Production Manager 2006 Andrew Coulton
Production Manager 2007 Liam Boucher

Marketing and Projects Officer Helen Black
Education Officer Angela Smith
Production Support Citizens' Theatre Company

TAG Theatre Company
www.tag-theatre.co.uk   **CITIZENS THEATRE**

Characters

Lee

Leila

Billy

Frank

Holly

YELLOW MOON

The Ballad of Leila and Lee

Police officer how can it be
You can arrest everybody
But cruel Stagger Lee,
That bad man, O cruel Stagger Lee.

Mississippi John Hurt
'Stack O Lee Blues'

'If you took all the clothes off all the people in
Cambridge,' declares Stuart, 'you'd be amazed
how many of them had scars.'

Alexander Masters
Stuart, a Life Backwards

ONE

Meet Lee Macalinden.
Meet Lee Macalinden's hat.

Lee Macalinden is seventeen and he lives with his mother in the Chapel Terrace Flats. We've always known Lee and we've always known Lee's hat because he's been wearing it since he was five years old and he never takes it off. We don't know which came first – the hat or the nickname.

Stag.

Stag Lee.

Everybody knows Stag Lee Macalinden. The police know him, the social work department know him, the children's panel, the school guidance teacher, the learning support staff, the doctor, the community council and the youth workers at the youth club in the Church, everybody knows Stag Lee.

He's a celebrity.

Lee's mum brings up Lee on her own because Lee's dad left when Lee was five.

Lee's mum gets regular visits from a feeling she calls the black dog. When the black dog visits her she goes to her bed with three bottles of vodka, a carton of cigarettes, and an old cassette tape of A-Ha's album *Hunting High and Low*.

She locks the bedroom door, puts the tape on, shuts the curtain, climbs into bed, drinks the vodka, and cries until the feeling of total and utter despair goes away.

Which can take a day or a month.

Or sometimes a year.

Last week Lee was expelled from school for using the art department computer to make fake pornographic pictures of the French assistant.

And then putting the pictures up on the school noticeboard.

During parents' evening.

'Lee will agree to respect school computer equipment. Lee's mum's boyfriend agrees to discuss with Lee issues of sexuality and proper respect for women. The school agrees to monitor Lee's behaviour and provide support through the guidance system.'

Did we mention Lee's mum's boyfriend?

This is Lee's mum's boyfriend discussing with Lee issues of sexuality and showing proper respect for women.

Billy   You are a catastrophe, Lee Macalinden, do you understand that? A fucking catastrophe. Look at yourself. You're a disgrace. Take that stupid hat off. Come here. Come here. I don't care about you or about your worthless life but your mother does and I love your mother. DO YOU UNDERSTAND THAT? I love your mother because she is an angel, DO YOU UNDERSTAND? And she is in there – my angel – in that room *weeping* because of you. Because she is worried about you, so despite my better instincts, I HAVE DECIDED TO TAKE AN INTEREST.

Meet Billy Logan.

Furniture salesman, Hearts fan and amateur boxer.

Billy Logan met Jenni Macalinden in the Volunteer Arms one night when she was working behind the bar. Billy came in with a stag party and he had a go on the karaoke.

Billy   'Take on me . . . take me on.'

Billy moved in with Jenni and Lee six months ago. He's even had a key cut. Now Billy wants to take the relationship onto a new level.

Billy   Candles. Bottle of wine. Chicken curry. Special. Here's ten quid. Go and get yourself a fish supper and a copy of *Razzle*. I don't want to see you back till after midnight. You understand me?

Billy's bought a ring.

TWO

Meet Leila Suleiman.

Leila Suleiman doesn't say much.

She's famous for not saying much.

That's her thing.

Most people just assume she's quiet because she's Muslim.

The way she dresses is Muslim, isn't it?

Maybe Muslim girls aren't allowed to speak.

Maybe she can't speak English.

Most people don't worry about it.

It's not as if we particularly want to ask her anything, is it?

Leila Suleiman gets good grades.

One day she will go to Aberdeen University to study English and she will most likely get a first because Leila Suleiman is a good girl.

Leila's dad is a doctor and her mum's a dentist. They came to Scotland in the 1990s. They were refugees from some sort of war. They live in a nice house in Hill Street which has a big garden with an apple tree and a view of the Forth.

On the walls in Leila's room there's a ceramic statuette of a wild horse galloping across a prairie, a postcard of the Great Mosque in Damascus and a selection of comical pictures of kittens.

There's one where a kitten is balancing on top of a dog.

And one where a kitten has cream on its whiskers.

Leila's staring at that picture right now. She's supposed to be doing homework but her mind is drifting. If we could hear the thoughts inside Leila's head we'd hear this:

This hand doesn't belong to me.
This arm doesn't belong to me.
I'm not here.
If I sit still enough for long enough maybe I'll float up to the ceiling and then I could look down on my stupid ugly body self sitting there stupid and ugly

thinking:

It's Friday night.
It's Friday night.
It's Friday night.

THREE

It's Friday night and Lee Macalinden is mooching about the living room in Chapel Terrace trying to work out how he could make big money from a life of crime.

Billy's making curry.
Jenni's locked herself in her room again.
It's dark outside.

And Lee's bored.

When he finds a wee box on the mantelpiece.

A wee box with a silver ring in it.

Result.

Lee Macalinden takes Billy Logan's silver ring into town and pawns it for a couple of hundred quid. Then he goes to visit his friend Fraser Harris,

Also known as H-Bomb,

Who sells him some dope some of which they smoke as they discuss ways in which Lee can make big money from a life of crime before Fraser Harris gets tired of Lee and chucks him out at eight o'clock. The police tell us that between eight p.m. and nine p.m. Lee sits on the wall outside the community centre making stupid comments to passers-by. At nine o'clock Lee goes in to the Happy Friar Fish Bar where he buys chips, plays on the fruit machine and attempts to buy a bottle of Thunderbird wine before telling all the women in the fish queue about his big idea for making money from a life of crime. At ten p.m. Mrs Kate Francetti, the owner, throws Lee out and he decides to go shoplifting from the all-night superstore instead.

Which is where, the police tell us, he met Leila Suleiman by the magazine racks on the night of 22nd January last year at exactly ten-fifteen p.m.

The night Billy Logan got murdered.

FOUR

It's Friday night.
It's Friday night.
It's Friday night.

Every Friday night Leila Suleiman goes down to the all-night superstore where she reads the celebrity magazines.

Leila loves the celebrity magazines.

She loves the names of them.

Closer. Heat. You. Now. More.

She loves the touch of them. She loves the colour of them and most of all she loves the feeling she gets when she reads them. For a little while on a Friday night Leila Suleiman doesn't live with us any more, she lives in a blurry universe of beaches and red carpets and handbag shops on Rodeo Drive and stables in Hampshire. Leila flicks through all the magazines in the rack until she finds just the right one with just the right pictures and then she goes to the checkout and buys a packet of disposable razors and some elastoplast whereupon she retires to the superstore toilets, removes one blade from its casing, puts the magazine over her knees, rolls up the sleeve of her blouse and draws the razor slowly across her forearm.

When Leila Suleiman cuts herself she feels like she is real. Like she's real like she's in a story. Like she's real like there's someone somewhere who wants to take a picture of her without her permission.

I'm here.
I'm here.
I'm here.

When the pain from the cut begins to ebb away Leila
finds that she is sitting in a toilet in Inverkeithing with
blood all over herself and tears in her eyes and that she's
once more stuck inside the ugliest stupidest person in a
world that doesn't really exist. She throws the rest of the
razors in the bin and swears to herself that she'll never
ever do something as ugly as that or as stupid as that ever
again.

She sticks a plaster over the cut,

Pulls down the sleeve of her blouse,

Wipes the tears from her eyes,

and walks back out into the shop and puts the magazine
back on the shelf where it belongs and goes home.

Which is what she was just about to do – only a moment
ago – when Lee Macalinden arrived in the shop.

The police showed us CCTV footage from the superstore
on the night of the murder and you can see Leila very
clearly, standing there, looking quite ugly and stupid
putting the magazine back on the shelf and then you see
at ten-fifteen p.m. a boy wearing a baseball cap come up
to her, unzip his flies and show her something inside his
trousers.

Lee   Hey Silent Leila,
        I've got a half-bottle of 20/20 down my pants.
        Do you want to come to the cemetery with me?
        . . .
        I'll let you share my chips.
        . . .
        I know they're cold but a chip's a chip.

Leila Suleiman thinks that going to the cemetery to drink 20/20 with Stag Lee Macalinden would, on balance, be a mistake.

Leila Suleiman is a good girl.

Leila Suleiman doesn't do that sort of thing.

Lee   Come on, you know you want to.

But when Stag Lee Macalinden walks away from her she watches him and she notices the way he moves through the shop as though he owns the place and so when he turns back to her and says:

Lee   Are you coming or are you coming?

Leila Suleiman hesitates.

In her heart at this moment there is a feeling she's only ever had twice before:

once praying in the Great Mosque in Damascus that day when she was twelve and God spoke to her and told her she was special in the manner of one day perhaps saving the world,

and the other time was that time in second year when she pulled her fingernails down the back of her hand during Mr Cochrane's Chemistry lesson.

A feeling like someone opening a door.

And now she has it again,

now right at this moment

looking at Stag Lee Macalinden's slight smile when he turns to her and says:

Lee   Are you coming or are you coming?

The CCTV footage shows Leila Suleiman leaving the shop with Lee Macalinden at ten twenty-one p.m.

FIVE

Meanwhile back at Chapel Terrace, Billy Logan is kneeling outside Jenni Macalinden's bedroom door with a pan full of burnt curry and an empty bottle of red wine.

Billy   Jenni.
Jenni.
Angel.
I can re-heat the curry.
Come out here please.
Jenni, are you listening?
Jenni.
COME OUT HERE NOW.
Jenni.
There's something important I've got to tell you.
Jenni.

Billy gets down on one knee. He opens the wee box and he sings:

     (*Sings.*) 'Take on me. Take on me.
     Take me on. Take on me.
     I'll be yours for ever more.'

And as Billy Logan sings, his song echoes down the stairwell of the Chapel Terrace flats and drifts out into the starlit frosty night where it floats across the town over the railway line up past the health centre and over the cemetery wall before finally dying away just yards from the bench where Stag Lee is sitting right now with Leila Suleiman outlining his big idea.

Lee   I'm thinking of going into business as a pimp.
I don't think there is a pimp in Inverkeithing at the moment. A pimp has to have ho's but I would have does, as in doe a deer. Because I'm Stag Lee.

He has worked out a rap.

> Stag, S.T.A. double G.
> Big and so hornee.
> Like Bambi's dad. I drive girls mad.
>
> I think there's room for a pimp in Inverkeithing.
> Roanna Castledine's agreed to be one my ho's.
> And so's Kerry Hunter, but I'd still be one ho
> short of the full back seat.
>
> . . .
> What do you say?
> Would you be one of my doe ho's, Silent Leila?
> There's lassies would give their right arms for
> some quality time with the Stag man. Check
> out these abs – (*He lifts his shirt.*) Check that
> out. I'm a prize.
> Check out these pecs.
> Go on.

Leila feels his heart thump under her hand.

She feels his heart beat faster.

And she wonders:

Did I make that happen?

Well did she?

No.

Billy   Lee.

It was not beauty that made Lee's heart beat faster.

Billy   Lee.

It was not Leila at all.

Billy   Lee.

It was a jilted amateur boxer with a score to settle.

Billy   Where's the ring?

Billy punches Lee in the stomach.

Lee   Where is it?

Billy pushes Lee.

Lee   Get off.

Billy pushes Lee again.

Billy   Where's the bloody ring?

Lee   Don't touch me.

Billy pushes Lee and this time Lee falls.

Billy   Get up.
          Get up and fight.

Lee stays down.

Billy   You think you're hard, Macalinden, but you're
          all front. You wouldn't last two minutes with
          me. Two minutes with me and I'd have you
          wetting your pants. Get up.

Lee stays down.

Billy   FIGHT.

Billy grabs Lee's hat.

Lee   Don't touch my hat.

Billy   Fight for it.

Lee   Give me the hat.

Billy   (*mocking*) 'Give me the hat.'

Lee   Don't touch my hat.

Billy   (*mocking*) 'Don't touch my hat.'

Lee takes out a knife and stabs Billy.

A pause.

Lee stabs Billy again.

Billy drops the hat.

Lee   I told you not to touch the hat.

Sometime between midnight and two o'clock in the morning on Saturday 23rd January Billy Logan felt his insides turn into blood and then, at almost the same moment, he felt the blood begin to drain away and his legs buckle beneath him.

Billy   Lee.

Somewhere between midnight and two o clock in the morning Billy Logan put his hands to his stomach.

His stomach felt wet and warm.

Somewhere between midnight and two in the morning Billy Logan died and as he died his mind was filled

With these words:

Cunt.
You cunt.
You fucking cunt.

Over and over again until the last of his breath was gone.

SIX

Midnight. We're shaking. We don't know what to do. What are we going to do? Let's just stand for a bit. Let's take Billy's wallet out of his inside jacket pocket. Let's pick up the knife. Let's just go. Let's just get out of here. Let's walk quickly out of the cemetery down onto the main road. Let's put our hoods up and keep our heads down. There aren't many cars anyway. Let's go past the

Comfort furniture store and then onto the coastal path by the bay. Let's go past the shipbreaker's yard and throw the knife over the wall. Let's walk on past the quarry through the woods to Port Laing beach. Let's go to Port Laing beach and let's make a small fire because it's cold and we're feeling a bit – well – we're feeling a bit shaky.

Let's sit close together and hold our hands out to the fire and let's think to ourselves we never want this moment to end because now, at last, we're in a story.

I'm here.
I'm here.
I'm here.

Leila and Lee probably sat by the fire till just before dawn on Saturday 23rd, when they would have seen the lights of the first freighter slipping out of the Forth on the morning tide and Lee must have wished he was on it. He would have thought about swimming out through the still water and climbing on board and signing up as a sailor or something and then – what?– He wouldn't have known what then. He would probably have turned to Leila and said something like –

Lee   I'll maybe go up north.
             Maybe go and see my dad.

Leila would have supposed that she should just go home.

Lee   You going to go to the cops?

Leila would have pondered the idea of telling the truth the whole truth and nothing but the truth but no –

Leila shakes her head.

She'd only have to talk.

Lee   What you going to do?

Leila would probably have supposed she could open her front door quietly and sneak into bed. She'd get away with it. She could go to school and pretend as if nothing had changed. She would probably have thought that was the thing she ought to do but then something must have happened. Leila saw something moving in the scrubby woods behind the beach, something alive in the dark.

And she watched

As a roe deer stepped out of the woods and onto the beach in front of her.

The deer sniffed

and turned

and looked at her.

Deer and girl, eyes locked for a second, two worlds trembling on the edge of the stillness, and then, silent as a thought, the deer stepped back into the woods and vanished just as if she'd never been there at all.

Deer Beach Fire Lee.

In that moment Leila Suleiman would have known that if she went home now she would feel so ugly and so stupid that she'd maybe actually have to throw herself off the Forth Road Bridge and Lee would have seen her smiling and he would have thought how surprisingly pretty she was which he'd never really properly noticed before and so he would maybe have said something like –

Lee   Do you want to come with me?
        Do you want to come up north?

Yes.

Lee must have explained that he had something he had to do first and he'd have told her to meet him at the station in time for the first train north and Leila would have gone back to the all-night superstore and bought a three-pack of pants, some toothpaste and toothbrush, a bag of apples.

Everything she needed to step into a new world.

What would Lee have had to do first?

He would most probably have gone to his mother
and sat beside her bed
and said something like:

Lee   Mum.
             I'm sorry.
             I stabbed Billy.
             I didn't mean to do it but I did.
             Mum.
             I've killed him.

             . . .

             I going to see my dad.
             He'll know what to do.
             Something like this.

             . . .

             Here's some money.
             Don't worry about me.

             . . .

             Will you be OK?
             Will you be OK just for a few days?
             Mum?

And if Jenni Macalinden could have screamed she would most probably have let out a scream that would have followed her son out of the door and down Chapel Terrace and chased him running all the way to Platform One, where it would have drowned out the noise of the Perth train clattering into the station.

But Jenni Macalinden wasn't able to scream.

So as he left

She just said:

Lee.

Which he wouldn't have heard as he shut the door behind him.

SEVEN

Seven in the morning and we're waiting at the station.

Plastic bag.

Commuters all around us.

Can't stop shivering.

Maybe he's not going to come.

Apples. Pants. Toothpaste.

Maybe the whole thing never happened.

Razors.

Maybe Billy Logan has sucked the blood back up into himself, brushed the dust off his suit and gone off to work at the furniture shop just like normal.

Razors.

Maybe we don't exist.

We need razors.

Maybe we're not here.

We need magazines.

Maybe we're not in a story at all, maybe nobody's imagining what it's like to be us, maybe we're just standing in our stupid ugly shoes on Inverkeithing station platform with everybody looking at us thinking:

Stupid.

Ugly.

Stupid.

Ugly.

Ten minutes past seven.

In five minutes exactly our mother will wake up.

She will open our bedroom door.

She will look at our bed unslept in.

She will see that the room is empty.

And she will say:

Leila.

More.

Closer.

Heat.

Now.

You.

The man in the kiosk is looking at us.

It's too late.

The Inverness train clatters into the station.

Where is he?

Lee   Leila.

There,

Walking down the platform like he owns it.

Lee   Leila.
           Are you coming or are you coming?

And suddenly everything is real again.

Suddenly everything's all right.

EIGHT

This is the part of the story where Leila and Lee go on the run to the highlands and nearly die.

A hundred years from now people'll tell this bit, and when they do it'll go like this:

They take the Perth express
Then change for Inverness
They'll get out of this mess.

The guard shouts tickets please
Hide in the lavatories
Avoid the fare with ease.

All right, all right
Maybe
Everything is all right.

Lee   My dad was a gangster.

Lee's holding a postcard.

Lee   He was the king of Glasgow.
           He made money.
           And he never got caught.

It's a postcard of the Highlands.
Mountains. Forest. Loch.
In the middle of the picture – a house.

Lee   That's his house.
           Must be about fifty rooms.
           He's got his own boat.
           He's got his own lake.
           Got his own forest.
           Got his own mountain.

The postcard's soft from the amount of times it's been held.

Lee   He sent this to my mum a few years ago. She
        keeps it in her pants drawer. I found it one day
        when I was looking for fags.

Dear Jenni, I don't know if this'll reach you. I don't
suppose you're still in the same place any more. Maybe
you're married. I've gone back up north like I always said
I would. Ha ha. I'm well set up here and nobody knows
who I am so nobody bothers me which is good. Here's
some money for the boy. Don't try to get in touch. Dan.

Lee   Dan.
        That's my dad's name.
        Blackwaterside.
        That's where we're going.
        Blackwaterside
        'Nr Kinlochewe.'
        Nr means near.

All right, all right
Maybe
Everything is all right.

Three hours stuck on the train
These hills all look the same
Leila's still glad she came.

Lee's bored, he wants some fags
Goes nicking from handbags
Works out his top ten shags.

All right, all right
Maybe
Everything is all right.

Inverness. They find a place to stop
The doorway of Top Shop
Lee puts his hand down Leila's top.

Night's black, too cold to sleep
Leila thinks she's in too deep
As you sow so shall you reap.

Lee   How come you don't say much, Silent Leila?
How come you don't speak?

Leila   I don't speak because most people aren't worth
speaking to.

Lee   Did you always not speak or did you just stop
one day?

Leila   I stopped one day. I was sitting on the wall at
school and Mr Hopeton passed me and he said,
'Everything all right, Leila?' And I looked at
him, and he said it again: 'Everything all right?'
And he smiled at me and I like Mr Hopeton so
I thought, 'I don't know, is everything all
right?' It seemed such a complicated question.
I didn't know. I didn't answer and eventually he
just said, 'Oh well. Good good.' And I realised –
people hear what they want to hear, it doesn't
matter what you say. So I just decided to stop.
I stopped bothering.

Lee   What about school?

Leila   I do my work. I don't cause any trouble.
Teachers have got far worse problems to deal
with than me.

Lee   Just silent. Just –

Leila   It's just easier.

Lee   Why did you come with me, Silent Leila?

Leila   Because . . .
Because when I'm with you I feel like I'm real
and I'm in a story and people are imagining
me and wondering what I think which is a

feeling I've only ever got from cutting myself
and just once that time in the Great Mosque
in Damascus when I thought I met God . . .

Of course she didn't really say that.
She didn't really say any of that.
She hardly even thought it, she was too busy looking at
him in the soft light of the Top Shop window display and
wishing he'd lift up his shirt and let her put her hand on
his heart again.

This is what actually happened.

Lee   How come you don't say much, Silent Leila?
           How come you don't speak?

Silence.

           Did you always not speak or did you just stop
           one day?

Silence.

           What about school?

Silence.

           Just silent. Just –

Leila smiles.

           Why did you come with me, Silent Leila?

First train at six-fifteen takes them to Achnasheen
Leila in a lovely dream
Best place she's ever been.

Lee makes friends with a local ned
Hotwires an old moped
Leila wishes she was dead.

Dump the bike in Kinlochewe
Not quite sure what to do.

Lee   Hey, hey, mister. Do you know how to get to
               Blackwaterside from here?

Lee shows the postcard:

>   Blackwaterside.
>   'Nr Kinlochewe.'
>   Nr.
>   Means near.

Man   Next glen. There's no road in. You got a four-
               by-four or something?

Lee   Moped.

Man   Path's over the hill. It's some walk, mind.
               You're better waiting till tomorrow. Frank the
               keeper comes into town for supplies on a Friday.
               He'll maybe give you a lift in the Land-Rover.

Lee   We'll walk.

Frozen halfway up the hill
Walking's not their greatest skill
Bleeding feet soon start to kill.

Four hours up a muddy track
Snow blowing at their back
Lee says fuck it, let's go back.

Don't know which way to go
Both walking really slow
Lee falls down in the snow.

Lee   I'm cold.

All right, all right
Maybe, maybe
Everything is all right.

Leila's too tired to try
No energy left to cry
Sit down and wait to die.

Lee	Cold.
Leila	I'm here.
	I'm here.
	I'm here.

A gunshot.

NINE

| Lee | What the hell was that? |

A gunshot again.

Frank.

The Keeper.

Out stalking deer.

He's seen them in the mist.

Frank	What the hell are you doing up here? Did you not read the sign at the path head. NO WALKING. Christ, look at the state of you. No boots? No waterproofs? Are you trying to get yourself killed?
Lee	We're lost, mister.
Frank	Lost.
	You're certainly lost.

Meet Frank.

Frank	You look a mess.
	You must be freezing.
	Take some of this.

He offers them both a drink from a hip-flask.

Also known as –

Lee   What is it? Tea?

Both take it and cough.

– Drunk Frank.

Frank   Whisky.
It'll warm you up.

Frank tells Leila and Lee to follow him. He leads them over the pass in the snow and mist, mouths still burning from the bite of the whisky and shaking with a wet cold gone deep into their bones. They scramble down a rocky slope, slithering and skittering and sending stones the size of fists bouncing down into the mist below till Frank stops on a patch of grass below a crag. He kneels down.

Frank   Here.

A dead deer.

Frank   You were lucky I was stalking today. I wouldn't normally be out on the hill a day like today but it's coming to the end of the season and I've hinds to cull.

Big red hole in the deer's head.

Two black glassy eyes looking up at them.

Frank   Give us a hand.

They drag the still warm beast a hundred yards or so up the hill to the hidden entrance of a small cave at the foot of some crags. Frank pulls the deer inside the cave. Into the shelter, out of the wind.

Frank   Sit down.

Frank takes out a large knife and kneels down by the deer and stabs the knife into its soft white stomach. Then he pulls the knife up the beast's body and with three sharp tugs he opens her up.

Frank   Here – get yourself warm. Put your hands
inside.

Lee   What?

Frank   Inside the wound.
Blood's still hot. Guts will warm your hands.

The wound looks black and it stinks.

Frank   Just do it.

They kneel and put their hands in the hot wet stomach
cavity of the dead hind.

The steam rises off Frank's jacket from the heat of his
body. They notice the steam of their breath and the hot
iron smell of blood rising out of the deep red wound
sucking at their hands.

Frank   I always keep a few supplies up here. Oatcakes.
Sweets. Matches. A couple of bottles. It's my
bolthole. Keepers here have used it for years.

He offers them more whisky.

Frank   Be dark in a couple hours.
I'll take you down the hill.
Get you some dry gear.
Then we'll work out how to get you home.

Lee   I don't want to go home, mister. I've come here
to find my dad.

Frank   Who's your dad?

Lee   Dan Macalinden.
He lives here.
Blackwaterside.
'Nr Kinlochewe.'
Nr means near.

Frank   You won't find Dan Macalinden here, son.

Lee   How not?

Frank   Dan Macalinden's dead.

There's sweat and snowmelt running down the keeper's
face that makes it look like he's crying but he isn't.
There's snowmelt running down Lee's face too. Lee
doesn't say anything. Leila listens to the wind and the
snow and breath from their bodies and she finds Lee's
hand amongst the blood and grips it.

He takes his hand away. Wipes his face. Blood on his face.

Frank   You're lucky. Lucky I found you. Another
couple of hours and you'd have been dead.

TEN

Drunk Frank took us down the hill in the argo with the
dead hind lolloping across our knees. Its head looking up
at us, its eyes glass and all the light gone out of them.
The jeep bumped down the track off the hill through the
black wood and finally coming out of the trees we see the
house. A big old place with turrets and towers – just like
in the postcard.

Lee   Is that my dad's house – was this his place?

Frank   That's right, son.

In the hanging shed we stood among the bodies of the
culled hinds. Frank laid out the beast for its butchery.
First he sawed off the head, then the legs, and then he cut
open its breastbone and pulled out the heart and lungs
and liver and kidneys. Then he hung the beast up with
the others and hosed it down with cold water. Then
Frank walked right up to me, he was holding something
in his hand.

Frank Here.

Something warm and wet and –

Frank Present.

I held the beast's heart still warm. I've never seen a heart of anything before. I held it a little away from me.

Frank What's the matter? Scared of a bit of meat and blood?

Frank laughed.

I'm not scared
I'm not scared.

You try drawing a razor across your arm, laughing man, and then you tell me that I'm scared of meat and blood.

Frank Veggie, are you?

I took the heart up to my mouth and I bit into it. Took a scrap off it. Swallowed it. I wiped the blood from my mouth.

Frank laughed again.

He took the heart from me and threw it in the bin with the rest of the pluck.

Lee looked at me.

I smiled at him.
Frank looks at us.

Frank Can you work?

Lee Maybe.

Frank You're in trouble. I don't know what kind of trouble it is, but it must be bad to send you up a mountain in the middle of winter. I could drive you to the cop shop in Inverness but I'm busy – I've got a cellar to fill with chopped logs and thirty more hinds to cull before the first paying guests come. You can make yourself useful for a few days till the heat dies down.

Lee And then what?

Frank Then you can fuck off back to wherever it is you come from and I won't say anything to anyone.

Lee How much an hour?

Frank Nothing an hour.

Lee That's blackmail.

Frank That's the deal.

Frank gives Lee the big knife.

Frank There's six hinds there needing hung – skinned, hung and the pluck taken out. You've seen how to do it.

As Frank walked away Lee threw a curse at him but I noticed something. Something about the way Frank walked. He was only the keeper of Blackwaterside but Drunk Frank, he walked through it as though he owned the place.

Lee This is supposed to be my dad's mansion.

We slept that night in the ghillies' caravan.

Lee My dad was supposed to sort things out.

I lay on my bunk in jeans and a jumper under a thin downy that smelt of sweat.

Lee I was thinking jacuzzis, you know, a room, a double bed.

The small electric heater made an orange light.

Lee   Maybe even some booze, maybe some drugs, maybe some girls.

Outside the caravan window, I could see the black wood.

Lee   'Cos my dad was the king of Glasgow.

A full yellow moon made the trees look cast in gold.

Lee   My dad was hard as stone.

Yellow moon made Lee's face seem cast in gold.

Lee   This was supposed to be the lap of luxury. The lap. The very lap.

Yellow moon makes a glint of gold in Lee's eyes.

Lee   Are you cold, Silent Leila?

Leila shakes her head.

Lee   Come in here with me?

Leila shakes her head.

Come on.

She shakes her head.

Do it.

She shakes her head.

Get warm.

She shakes her head.

Bodily warmth.

She shakes her head.

I'm going to make you speak, Silent Leila.
One day I'm going to make you speak
And the first words you're going to say
Will be
Thank you, Lee, for that fine orgasm.

31

ELEVEN

Frank   Up! Up! Up!

Lee   You've got to be joking.

Six o'clock the next morning.

Frank has them chopping logs before breakfast –

Lee   I should at least be on the minimum wage.

– and clearing gutters after.

In the afternoon they paint the boat and at night they take hay out onto the hill to feed the deer.

Lee   This is actual fascism.

Lift stuff. Move stuff. Tidy stuff. Cut stuff and wash stuff.

Stuff needs fixed. Stuff needs cleaned.

For a place with no people
there's a hell of a lot of stuff.

In the evening, Frank hands Lee a big slab of meat to cut up. Lee takes one look at it:

Lee   What's this?

Frank   Venison.

Lee   What's that?

Frank   Deer.

Lee   Deer?

Frank   Cut it up. Peel carrots. An onion. Make a stew.

Lee   Disgusting.

Frank   Don't eat it, then.

Lee	I won't.
Frank	Suit yourself.
Lee	Not touching any more of this slop.
Frank	Cheerio.
Lee	I'm not working for nothing.
Frank	Don't then.
Lee	You're taking the piss.
Frank	Yes, I am.
Lee	I'm not stopping here.
Frank	Good.
Lee	Are you coming or are you coming?
	. . .
	Fuck off then.

Lee slams the door.

Frank   He'll be back. It's cold. Long walk to the road.

Leila makes the stew. They eat it. It's all right. Frank tells Leila to do the dishes.

Frank opens a bottle.

They sit by the fire.

Frank puts a record on.

Frank   Three things black I like in the world, Leila: the black wood, Johnnie Walker Black Label and black music

Frank wonders if he should tell Leila the story of the first time he heard this song. How his mate Gibby took him to the Glasgow Blues and Folk club at the Art School in 1985 because he said Art School girls were easy, nothing to do with the music. The draw was some old black guy they'd brung over from New Orleans and he was playing the guitar like he had twenty-five fingers but in the crowd there was a girl. She was dressed all in black and she was listening to song as though it had taken over her whole body.

Frank was wearing a maroon jumper and white jeans and he had casual's hair flicked across his eyes. He didn't like students but he liked the music. He liked the music a lot. Then the girl looked at him and she smiled.

So Frank buys the girl a drink.

And you know, they went back to her place and he rolled a couple and the girl asked him who he was and what he did and all the usual questions and something about her or the music or was it just that magic thing that sometimes happens between people but Frank decided to do the one thing he would never normally do with anybody and he told her the truth. He told her about how he came from up north where his dad was a keeper but he'd run away from home because the old man was a bastard to him and he'd been in and out of Polmont a couple of times for fighting but now he stayed with Gibby, mostly selling speed or dope, sometimes he did a robbery if Gibby's mate Jester organised things but actually if truth be told he wasn't a bad man.

If truth be told he was lost.

And the girl looked at him in the dark of a bedsit somewhere just off on the Great Western Road sometime in 1985 and she says:

Well you're not lost any more.

I've found you.

And Frank remembers the night they spent together and how, in the morning, he asked her, 'What about you? Are

34

you a blues fan?' And the girl said no. She was only at
the club because her boyfriend took her. She liked to
dance. She liked A-Ha.

A mile and a half down the track in the dark Lee sits on a
stone and rolls a cigarette, can't see a hand in front of his
face, lights it, a flame in the dark, thinks of his mother
and thinks of his father, looks out into the black wood and
lets the dark draw him in until he's just a thought floating
on a sea of the night and it's as if he's never existed.

Frank looks at Leila listening to the record and he wonders
if he should tell that story. He wonders if she would
understand.

But the night's passed now and the bottle's drunk and the
song's still clicking in its groove and Frank doesn't
understand himself any more so instead he just asks her:

Frank   Silent Leila, do you like to dance? Do you like
         A-Ha?

And falls asleep.

Lee   It's cold out there.
         Still a bit of heat from that fire.
         He finished a bottle of whisky.
         Old bastard.
         I'm going to bed.
         Early start tomorrow.
         Are you coming or are you coming?

TWELVE

They work on the estate for three months.

To tell you the truth Frank's not much up to the job. He's
hungover in the morning. His hand shakes too much to
use the saws or the axes. He's forgetful and does the same

35

job twice. He dozes. By ten-thirty he's usually sharpened up and he makes the plans for the day, does the really important stuff, but by four or five in the afternoon he's on the road to drunk again.

Frank needs them.

And Leila and Lee learn keepering fast. Frank shows them how to coppice the wood. They learn which tree's which. How to lay a path. Strip an engine. Build a fire. Shoot a fox. Tell the weather.

Weeks go by and they don't see another human being.

You'd hardly notice Leila didn't speak.

Because while they're at Blackwaterside

nobody speaks much.

Except in the evening when Frank puts on old blues records and late late in the evening when he's drunk and slurring his words and he'll put his hand on Leila's knee or Lee's shoulder and say:

Frank   Listen to that.

And:

Frank   That says it all.

And:

Frank   It doesn't go away.

And:

Frank   You wouldn't understand.

And:

Frank   I'm sorry. I'm sorry.

Leila and Lee sit on the sofa trying not to laugh. Frank's head nods.

He falls asleep
And the record clicks in the groove.

They had almost forgotten why they were at
Blackwaterside.

They had almost forgotten Billy Logan.

They had almost forgotten everything about that other
world.

That other world out there over the hills.

That other world which doesn't exist.

Until the night the Land-Rovers came.

THIRTEEN

It feels like spring's coming.
Imagine it's late in the evening and you're lying in your
bunk awake and Lee says:

Lee   I want to look around my dad's place.
            Come on.
            Let's break in the big house and sneak around.
            We won't touch anything.

Imagine you're not sure about it. Frank's told you not to
go in there. Place seems spooky anyway. But imagine Lee
smiles and he says that thing.

Lee   Are you coming or are you coming?

And so you decide to go with him.

Lee spots an open window at the back of the house. You
both climb inside. The corridors are dark. Lee switches a
torch on and the beam cuts into the dark. Walls panelled
in dark wood. Paintings everywhere. Abstract paintings.
Modern sculptures. Glass vases. You've never seen

anything like it. This is a house where every object, every corner on which your eye could settle is perfect. Like you're walking through the pages of *Hello*. Imagine you come to a huge room at the top of the house. The room's full of deer heads and gold mirrors and African shields and swords as though it was a museum. And Lee sits in a chair and looks into the dark.

Lee   My dad must have walked down these corridors.
            He must have looked at those mad paintings,
            he must have chosen them. He must have sat in
            this chair looking at them. He must have sat
            in this chair and looked out of that window at
            that hill and he must have thought, this belongs
            to me. This is me. Look at me. Look the fuck
            at me. He must have sat here in this chair and
            looked out of the window at that hill and he
            must have thought about me.
            He sat here and he thought about me.

And you think to yourself, imagine if this was real? What if it was real that we were here in this room in this place, what if it was real that we were in *Hello* magazine, what if this moment was real?

And imagine Lee finds a really old-fashioned record player.

Lee   Check this out.

And imagine beside the record player is a stack of old 45 singles.

Lee   Check this.

Imagine he picks the top one off the pile and plays it.

And imagine it's this song:

    The Chantels, 'Maybe'.

They dance, have fun,

They very nearly kiss.

Suddenly the room is lit by two great beams of light and the sound of revving engines as two black Land-Rovers swing into the courtyard.

Lee   Let's get out of here.

The Land-Rover door opens and a woman steps out.

Lee   Come on.

Imagine you recognise her.

Lee   You get caught if you want to. I'm getting out of here.

Imagine you recognise the woman because she's famous and you read about her every week in celebrity magazines. Imagine she's called Holly.

Holly Malone.

And imagine Holly Malone is walking towards the door of Blackwaterside Lodge with an entourage behind her of her secretary, her personal assistant, her chef and her bodyguard. The bodyguard opens the lodge door and Holly steps inside. She turns and looks along the dark corridor and she sees you. You stand still. You look at each other. Your two worlds tremble on the edge of stillness. And then, as silently as a thought, you're gone and Holly thinks that she must have imagined a girl, or perhaps that it was true what her manager said about Blackwaterside, that it was haunted.

OK, Let's jump ahead. Frank's woken up. You and Lee are standing in the kitchen feeding him coffee and Nurofen.

Frank   Shit. Damn. Blast. Shit. Shit. Damn.

He's still drunk but he's sobering up fast.

Frank	I forgot to write the dates in my diary. She's some friend of Mr de Vries. She's staying a week. Did she see you?
Lee	No.
Frank	Fuck. You're not supposed to be here.
Lee	Where can we go?
Frank	You'll have to sleep in the woods till I sort it out.
Lee	What?
Frank	So they don't see you. If she tells de Vries I could lose my job.
Lee	We can't sleep in the woods.
Frank	You'll be fine.

Imagine you and Lee put your heads down and your hoods up and you walk across the courtyard and into the black wood in the dark. You walk slowly. You go quietly. You know the way now. You can hear the voices of the celebrity party floating up from the big house. You can hear the shush of the wind in the pines. You can hear your own breath under your hood. High up on the hillside you start to make a fire the way Frank's taught you. And the flame catches the tinder and it lights and you sit down next to each other in the dark.

You feel like your bodies are full of electricity. Feeling like you'll crackle if you touch.

Lee's stolen a bottle of whisky from Frank's supplies.

Lee	Dutch courage.

What does Lee need courage for?

Lee   Silent Leila, see what happened in the house?

What happened in the house?

Lee   Where we nearly – we nearly –

Oh that.

Lee   Did you mean it?

You meant it.

Lee   I – I – I want to – should I –?

Imagine Lee – Stag Lee – Inverkeithing's only pimp – is
stammering.
Imagine he's nervous.
Imagine that.

He puts his hand onto your hip and under your T-shirt
but he's anxious, he moves too fast. It's like he's impatient.
He puts his hand up your top but you move it away
because you want him to slow down. He puts his hand
between your legs but you move it away because you just
want him to breathe, calm and slow, and then he says:

Lee   Do you want me to finger you? I know how to
            finger girls – I know a thing, I saw a thing –
            I want to push you down – Just rough like I'm
            in charge – I'm going to push you down –
            I don't want to push you down – outdoor sex is
            sexy for girls – Are you a virgin? Up against a
            tree – take a picture. I want to put it – to put it –
            right – to – fucking – I want – can't say it – I
            should have gone down on you – that's what
            I should have – you want someone better than
            me – you want someone who knows what to
            do – I don't know what to do – I don't know
            what you want – What do you want, silent
            Leila?

Leila   Take off your clothes.

| Lee | You spoke. |
| Leila | Do it. |

Lee takes off his clothes.
He is a prize.
You take off your clothes.
Lee sees your body
Old cuts like tribal markings.
And he touches you.
You are a prize.
Imagine what that would be like.

That's what it was like.

FOURTEEN

Leila wakes up with the dawn. She looks across the embers of the fire and she sees Lee, lying in his sleeping bag, dead to the world. Leila feels as if they're in a special bubble of time, time away from time, a bubble of real time only for them. She climbs out of her sleeping bag and scrambles down through the woods to the lochside. She stands on the pebbled beach in her bare feet and underwear. She looks out at the water and the mountains. She steps into the loch. The freezing water makes her gasp for breath and then, in the soft milk light of the morning, she swims.

Far away from herself.
Far away.

Holly	You.
	Hey you.
	You there.

Holly
Standing on the shore
Waving.

Holly   I saw you swimming. I saw you from my
          bedroom window. It looked so nice I wanted to
          come and join you. I put on my bathing costume.
          I saw a bird flying over the lake. It's just amazing.
          Isn't it just amazing? Can I come in?

Holly walks into the loch.

          Oh.
          Oh God it's really –
          Oh God that's cold, I can hardly –
          I can hardly stand to.
          Do you get used to it?
          I suppose you get used to it eventually.
          You get used to it.
          Can I swim to you?
          Can I swim with you?

Holly spins and whoops in the water as she gets used to
the cold. Her voice echoes off the mountains. Holly holds
her nose and ducks her head under the black water and
for a second Leila hears the quiet before Holly surfaces
and exhales like a seal rising.

Holly   You must belong to the cottage.
          Do you speak English?
          . . .
          It's very pretty here.
          The mountains.
          The forest.
          I feel so happy.

She swims to Leila.
She swims this close.

Holly   You're very pretty.
          You're so normal.
          I wish I was normal.
          We could be friends.

Do you know who I am?
. . .
I feel bored.
Are you bored?
I'm cold.
Are you cold?
Let's go in.

They swim to the shallower water and find their feet on the slippery rocks. They stumble out onto the beach.

Holly   I can't feel my feet.
I can't feel my fingers.
I can't feel anything.

Leila walks out of the water and she sees Holly's body.
She sees cuts.
All down the top of her thighs.
Cuts like tribal markings.
Holly sees Leila's body.

Holly   Come with me.

Holly takes Leila into the big house, up to the room like a museum and they sit by the fire.

Holly   Isn't this weird?
Us being in this room together.
Like two strangers in a reality show.
If this was a reality show,
You would be my friend.

I wish this was a reality show.
I wish he would come back to me.
I wish they liked me.
I wish I could sing.
I wish.
I wish I was you.
I wish you were me.

Leila watches Holly Malone as she puts a record on the turntable and

In the soft light of the morning

Holly cuts herself.

FIFTEEN

I don't have a story for that last week.
The time of the fire.
The time of the cave.
The time of being so happy.
The time of the chase.
I only have the jumble of pictures in my head
And questions
And none of it makes sense.

Let's start with the fire.

Lee   Watch out!

A wall of flame six feet high is coming down the hillside towards Leila. She can feel the heat on her face like a blast of air off an oven door.

It's the time of the Muirburning.

Leila and Lee are beating down a heather fire on the hillside. Early part of the summer, the keepers set fire to some of the heather to burn it back.

You need a few days dry before you start so the ground burns well. You set the fire and then beat it back to stop the fire spreading out beyond where you want it. Beyond where you've planned it to go.

Frank   I'll set the fires here. Once the fire's covered enough ground I'll give you the signal, you two beat it out.

Lee	What then?
Frank	Then we start another fire. Fun, eh?
Lee	Jesus.

Flames all around me coming towards me.
I'm fighting.

All the strength she's got thrown against the fire.
Again and again.

I'm surprised how strong I am.
Fire moves like it's alive.
Runs away from us.
Runs towards us.
Changes its mind on a turn of the wind.
Roars like a dog and turns to bite us.

Every time I beats it down.
My face soot black.
Sweat in my eyes and I think
This has to be the last one, I can't do any more.

Frank	Faster, you two, come on. It's getting the better of you.
Lee	Are you coming or are you coming?

A new wall, a big wall, bigger than the others, six-foot,
seven-foot sheet of flame dances towards me.

Lee	Smoke in my throat.

I think Lee's holding his hat – maybe he's trying to wave
the smoke away – he must be holding it because

a gust of wind and a punch of flame.

Lee's hat goes in the fire.

Frank	Leave it.

The wall of flame passes over it.

Lee   It's going to burn.

Frank   Leave it, son.

Lee   I want my hat.

Frank   Leave it.

I can see the picture of myself –

I step into the wall.

A picture of myself stepping through

Into the flames.

A circle around me now.

And I reach down to the heather and pick up the hat.

And then there's flame around me and Lee sees that I'm caught so:

Lee   Leila.

Frank   Shit.

Lee jumps through the wall.
The two of us now
two bodies
two breaths
two flames in a world of flames.

The blue sky above us
The wet peat below us and all around us fire.
Nothing in our heads but fire.

And when it's died. When all around us is the blackened moor. We stand there. Covered in soot and smoke.

Black
Like two burned trees.
Good as new.

I have a picture of us sitting at the end of the day coloured red by the sunset. We're holding beer. Did Frank bring the beer? It was cold. He must have put it into the stream. We sit among the ash and smoke on two hot rocks by the stream and watch the sun go down.

Please please please let it always be like this.

Please let that be the end. The three of us on the soot-black rocks and in my head we're red, lit red by the red sunset and watching the loch shimmer red like molten metal.

Please let that be the end of the story.

Please.

SIXTEEN

Lee   Frank.

Frank   Yeah?

Lee   My dad's not dead, is he?

Please let's not do this bit.

Lee   He's here.

Let's go back.

Lee   Isn't he?

Please.

Lee   He's you.

SEVENTEEN

So I'm caught.

You've worked it out.

What do you want me to say?

C'mere, son.

Let me give you a hug.

Is that what you want?

And now with the sky red and beautiful you're smiling at me and I'm thinking why did the sky have to go and be red and beautiful as if this was a story – it's not a story, it's a fuck up, Lee. And then you start talking.

Stop talking, Lee.

About how you saw the stag tattoo on my back that day when we were chopping the logs and how you noticed it was the same as the stag on your hat.

You're talking about how you've kept that hat all through your life.

I don't care.

How that's how come you've got the nickname 'Stag'.

I knew that.

You're telling me something about Jenni and some new man.

I don't want to know.

You're telling me about Jenni and this man and how you've been expelled from school.

Shut the fuck up, Lee, you talk, you always did talk.

And now you're telling me about how things are not good between you and this guy and so I nod, you know, serious, like a dad should nod, my eyes glistening with wise thoughts but I don't know what to say, Lee, I haven't got a clue.

And you're telling me about the cemetery.

Why are you telling me this?

About that night.

Don't tell me this.

About how you had a knife.

And

Now you say

I killed him,

Dad.

You say,

Dad.

I killed Billy Logan in the cemetery.

You say

He shouldn't have touched my hat.

Your hat,

Dad.

That's what you said.

One day, Lee, when you were five, I took you for a walk up Falkland Hill. We walked up through the oak forest over a carpet of dry leaves and as we climbed I taught you the 'Stag O Lee Blues'.

I lifted you up on to my shoulders and I imagined us in the future sitting on a rock in a red sunset looking out over a loch, sharing a beer and remembering that day on Falkland Hill. The day I taught you the 'Stack O Lee Blues'.

Should I ask if you remember that?
Should I ask you why you still wear the hat?

Are you crying?

Stop crying, Lee.
What do you want me to say?

It's all right?

It's not all right.

It's completely not all right.

Should I hold you?

Hold on to you?

I wonder if I should tell you the story of how one night when you were five and Gibby came round to play cards and he was winding me up about something and Jenni was giving me shit about something and I was off my tits on Jack Daniels and speed and Gibby said something else, something just to wind me up, and so I went into the kitchen, took a knife off the chopping board and stabbed him in the heart and he died. I wasn't aiming for his heart. It was a mistake.

I wasn't aiming for his heart. It was a mistake.

I wonder if should tell you that story.

But I can't remember what the point of it is any more.

I'm going to lose you, Lee.

Again.

And this time I'll never get you back.

So in the end Lee,

In the end,

I turn to you and this is what I say.

Frank   Why the fuck were you wearing that fucking
stupid hat?

EIGHTEEN

Lee's running down the mountain.

Frank just curled up on the rock like some dumb beast.

Crying and crying.

Leila hears a Land-Rover start up in the courtyard. Lee
must be stealing it. She hears it drive up the track away
from her. Leila wants to speak. She wants to say: put
down the whisky. Get up off your arse and go after him.
One of us has to fetch him back and I can't drive a Land-
Rover. She wants to make Frank realise. Get him. Fetch
him. But what can she say? Frank's going nowhere
tonight.

There's only one person on the estate with a driving
licence and car keys, who hasn't already tanked a bottle
of Bell's.

*Leila and Holly in a Land-Rover driving along the
track at night. They bump around. Holly drives very
fast.*

Holly   Catch Lee.
This is like a challenge in a reality show.
It's like there might be a prize.
. . .
Once I did a show
Where I drove a four-by-four
Through the desert.
I was voted off on the third day.
. . .

I'm like you.
I love the bad boys.
. . .
I don't care if I die.
Do you care if you die?
. . . .
You're so pretty.
Do you have a modelling contract?
Do you know who I am?
. . .
There he is.
That's him.
Let's get him.

Holly and Leila chase Lee through the night, over the narrow winding track. Their headlights cut great chunks out of the black sky. Lee drives fast but Holly drives better. She knows how to ease the four-by-four over the bumps and through the streams. Lee's only ever really driven a stolen Fiat Punto.

He takes a corner too fast and he turns over.

Rolls down a bank to the river.

Stops just before the water.

Holly and Leila stop, they turn the headlights down towards him.

Holly   He's all right.
Look, he's running.
. . .
Go.
Go and catch him.
Leila,
Catch him.
Catch your bad boy.

NINETEEN

Daily Record:

'Killer Teens In Highland Chase.'

'PC Gregor McCathie tells how a gruelling moorland pursuit ended in a grisly discovery.'

That isn't what happened.

Daily Mail:

'Goth Teen Satanist Death Pact.'

That isn't what happened.

Press and Journal:

'Teenage Knife Couple Caught after Chase.'

No.

The Herald.

'Upmarket Highland Lodge Blackwaterside was the unlikely venue yesterday for a full-scale police search operation.'

No.

'Police received a tip-off from the gamekeeper about the whereabouts of teenage murder suspect, Lee Macalinden.'

It didn't happen like that.

Lee ran. I chased him but he was too fast. I lost him in the dark. I walked back along the road to the cottage but Frank had gone. I found three notes.

To Mr de Vries:

'The lodge should be tidy and ready for the summer visitors. All the jobs are done on the hill. Sorry for any inconvenience I may have caused. Frank.'

To the Police:

'The boy is out on the hill. He's unarmed. I have the only shotgun. He is a good boy. Everything that happened was a mistake. Everything that happened was my fault.'

To Lee:

'I'm sorry.'

TWENTY

Daytime.
A cave on the hillside.

Lee sits cradling a shotgun.
Frank's dead body sits nearby, propped up against the wall of the cave.

Leila enters.
She sees Frank and gasps.

She goes to touch him.
He points the gun at her.
She stops.

Lee	Don't come near me.
Leila	It's OK. It's all right.
Lee	I'll shoot.
Leila	I'm on my own. I knew you'd be here.
Lee	I'm not coming out.
Leila	I know.
Lee	They can fuck off.
Leila	They don't know you're here.

Lee	Don't they?

Beat.

I want them to come in. Guns blazing. I'll take them out one by one by one, boom boom boom, till the fuckers' bodies are piled up like a wall and then one last pair of cartridges and boom-boom, bye-bye.

Leila	Everything's going to be all right, Lee. I promise.
Lee	Did they see you come in here?
Leila	They didn't see me.

Beat.

Leila	Poor Frank.
Lee	This is where I found him.
Leila	You been here all this time?
Lee	I went down to get whisky and got caught in the woods when the cops came. Did you tell them?
Leila	No.
Lee	Who told them?
Leila	He did.

Beat.

Leila	It's cold.
Lee	Shivering.
Leila	You wouldn't know it was June.
Lee	No.
Leila	More like February.
Lee	What way did you come?

Leila	Back of the hill track. There's police everywhere down by the house. They're all around the lochside.
Lee	I missed you.
Leila	Me too.

Lee nods. He shivers.

Leila	Watch the trigger, Lee.
Lee	Cold.
Leila	Give me the gun.
Lee	No.

Beat.

| Lee | He must have done it just after we left. He must have climbed up here in the dark. It was a full moon, wasn't it? Full yellow moon. He must've drunk a whole bottle. He must have sat here as the sun came up and looked out at the view. He must have sat here looking at the hills and he must have thought, this belongs to me. This is me. Look at me. Look the fuck at me. And then he must've pulled the trigger. Was he thinking about me? He must have been thinking about me. He must have been sitting here and he was thinking about me. |

Beat.

Leila	Give me the gun, Lee.
Lee	I can't.
Leila	Please, Lee.
Lee	I can't.

Beat.

Leila	I've worked it out, Lee. You'll never get murder for stabbing Billy. It was self-defence, Lee. I'll say it was self-defence. You'll get ten years, maybe even seven if you make a good impression on the judge and you'll make a good impression, Lee, I know you will, because you're not bad, Lee, you're good.
	. . .
	And if you get seven and you behave well and you keep your head down and maybe do an apprenticeship, maybe learn a trade, maybe do a degree, you could do a degree, Lee, you could be out in five years.
	. . .
	I'll go to university. I'll keep a photo of you by my bed. I'll write a book about us.
	. . .
	One day, a day that seems a million miles away now, but one day, a day that will come, Lee, one day you'll come out and I'll be standing outside the prison gates waiting for you.
	. . .
	We'll come back here. We'll drive up the track and I'll have bought Frank's cottage with the money from my books and you'll be the keeper and Holly Malone will own the big house and we'll all be one big happy family.
Lee	Your voice, Silent Leila.
Leila	What about it?
Lee	It's beautiful.
Leila	Put down the gun, Lee, please.

Beat.

Lee   Are we still –

Leila	Still what?
Lee	You and me.
Leila	Suppose so.
Lee	I didn't know.
Leila	If you want to –
Lee	I want to –

Leila moves in to kiss him.

I don't want to let go.

Leila takes control of the situation.

Leila	Slowly. Slow.
Lee	Slow.
Leila	Yes.
Lee	Slow.

A moment.
Lee stops.
He cocks the gun.

Lee	It's not going to work.
Lcila	What?
Lee	THIS. YOU. THIS –
Leila	What?
Lee	It's pointless.
Leila	No.
Lee	They're going to take me down. I'll go down for years and years and years. I'm dead. You saw Drunk Frank, Dan – Dad – my dad. Years

and years, man. I'll be old when I get out. Thirty. Forty. You'll be long fucked off with someone from college, some nice life, kids. Something. Some – some good life –

Leila   I promise I will wait for you.

Lee   Don't promise that.

Leila   I promise.

Lee   Don't make stupid promises.

Leila   Don't call my promises stupid.

Lee   Everything good gets taken away from me.

Leila   It doesn't get taken away, Lee, you throw it away.

Lee   I'll end up like him.

Leila   He loved you, Lee.

Lee   Some stupid bloody idiot who threw it all away.

Leila   He loved you but he wasn't very good at it. He thought love was supposed to look like the morning or something, all birds tweeting and sun in the blue sky, he wanted it to be like that, but love isn't like that, is it?

Lee   A stupid bloody idiot who threw it away.

He puts the gun in his mouth.

Leila   Do it then.
          Go on.
          Do it.
          Shoot.
          Throw it away.
          Coward.

Fucker.
FUCKER.
Do it.
Shoot.

He drops the gun.

Lee   I wish I could go back.

Leila   So do I.

Lee   I'm sorry about Billy.

Leila   So am I.

The massive sound of a helicopter approaching.

Lee   They've found us.

The helicopter is near.
The helicopter is very near.

Lee   There's something we've got to do.

Lee stands.

Lee pulls Frank's body in front of them.
He takes out a knife.

He stabs it into Frank's body, three sharp tugs and he opens him up.

Lee reaches into the wound and pulls out Frank's heart and holds it. They hold it together for a few moments. Then Lee digs a hole in the back of the cave and buries the heart and covers it with a stone.

Lee   Come on.

Leila   What about your hat?

Lee   Leave it.

He moves towards the entrance.

Lee   Are you coming or are you coming?

Helicopters become louder still as Leila and Lee leave the cave.

Music: Lloyd Price, 'Stagger Lee'.

End.